The Bungalow of Colorful Aging

The Bungalow of Colorful Aging

Poems by

Bruce W. Niedt

Cover design by Shay Culligan
Photo by José Alejandro Cuffia on Unsplash

ISBN: 978-1-63980-064-3

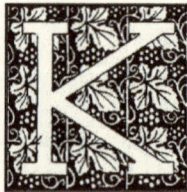

Kelsay Books
502 South 1040 East, A-119
American Fork, Utah 84003
Kelsaybooks.com

Acknowledgments

These poems, some in slightly different forms, first appeared in the following books and journals:

Aprilcalypse (author's chapbook, Four Feathers Press, 2020):
  "PM"

Boston Literary Magazine: "Deus ex Machina"

Chantarelle's Notebook: "After Seeing *Star Wars*," "The Back Door," "Last Spring," "Marginalia," "Mercurochrome Summer," "Papers on Top of More Papers," "Things in Need of Love," "When the Ghosts Came"

Edison Literary Review: "Handyman," "Sette Pesci," "The Stars Obliterated"

Global Poemic: "Aprilcalypse, 2020" (published as "Aprilcalypse")

Mad Poets Review: "Hoofing"

Mason Street Review: "How a Toddler Learns the Alphabet," "What's Fixed"

Plath Poetry Project: "Cedar"

Poem Your Heart Out (anthology, Words Dance Publishing, 2015): "Romantics"

Rattle: "The Man Peeling Sweet Potatoes on Easter Morning"

Schuylkill Valley Journal: "Insidious"

Spitball: "Last Spring," "Randy Johnson Kills a Bird"

Tiferet: "Möbius Avenue," "Start the Music"

Tilt-a-Whirl: "Careful in the Fog"

U.S. 1 Worksheets: "A Day in July," "Dewey-Eyed," "Interview with a Metaphor," "Nail Pop," "The Photo from M87," "Postcard to the Ex," "Rapids Again," "Señor Morning," "Shelter," "Trivia"

Verse Wisconsin: "Downsizing"

Writer's Digest: "Purple Heart," "Senior Discount"

Your Daily Poem: "Public Apology"

Thank you to all the poets and editors whose influence, guidance and support have made this book possible, including Jane Hirshfield, Marge Piercy, Billy Collins, Molly Peacock, Robert Lee Brewer, Kendall and Christinia Bell, Nancy Scott, Eileen D'Angelo, Gina Larkin, Peter Krok, Anna Evans, Mike Shannon, Vince Gotera, Celeste Schantz, and special thanks to Lorraine Stanchich Brown for her advice, copy-editing, and friendship. Finally, thanks as always to my family for their love and support.

Contents

Part I Where Words Come

Start the Music   13
The Flute Remembers   14
Marginalia   15
To a Famous Poet   16
Journal Evening (Loving Near June)   17
Romantics   18
Interview with a Metaphor   19
Archaics Roadshow   20

Part II Already Beginning to Heal

Mercurochrome Summer   23
Shelter   25
Aquaphobia   26
Hide and Seek   27
Science Fair Volcano   28
The Stars Obliterated   29
Things in Need of Love   30
Dewey-Eyed   31
A Day in July   32
Couch Nocturne   33
Trivia   34
Postcard to the Ex   35
Insidious   36
Public Apology   37
What's Fixed   38
The Agnostic's Sunday   39
PM   40

Part III A Certain Age

The Man Peeling Sweet Potatoes
    on Easter Morning   43
Sette Pesci   44
Rapids Again   46
Family Engagements   47
Hoofing   48
Handyman   49
How a Toddler Learns the Alphabet   50
Easter Egg Hunt in a Church Graveyard   51
After Seeing *Star Wars*   52
Senior Discount   53
Downsizing   54
Papers on Top of More Papers   55
Careful in the Fog   56
Nail Pop   57
Deus ex Machina   58
Señor Morning   59
Möbius Avenue   60
Aprilcalypse, 2020   61
In the Bungalow of Colorful Aging   62
Packing Old Records   63

Part IV Look Out, Look Out, Look Out

When the Ghosts Came   67
Cedar   69
Randy Johnson Kills a Bird   71
Burying the Gerbil   72
Purple Heart   73
Last Spring   74
Tribute to Flight 370   75
The Back Door   76
The Photo from M87   77

No wonder the moon in the window seems to have drifted out of a love poem that you used to know by heart.
—Billy Collins, "Forgetfulness"

Part I

Where Words Come

Start the Music

Be in a place where words come,

like a night hill above all the wash of lights
where you can lie on your back and make
your own constellations, where it's so quiet
you can hear the world turning on its axis,

or the middle of a Bach Brandenburg Concerto,
where you imagine yourself the cello,
and arpeggios resonate in your chest
and counterpoint embroiders the air,

or an early morning walk, when your steps
set the rhythm and a symphony of birds
set the melody, and only you and they know
what secrets the sun kept all night,

or a Coltrane sax solo growling in your ear buds,
a new animal birthed from the bell of his instrument
that carries you away on harmonics like a wisp
of smoke in that club where he used to play,

or your spring garden, where you sit under
your wisteria that's overripe with purple
clustered flowers, and the bees buzz
above you like some divine machinery.

Wherever it may be, it can only be your place,
and only your words can know how to get there.

The Flute Remembers

after "Ode to the Flute" by Ross Gay

And then a man
looks at a flute
beside him and asks,
"How did you learn
to catch the wind?"
and the flute
remembers a time
before silver and keys
that locked in the wind
and remembers days
of wood
and finger holes
and how people would
dance to its wind
the same wind
that has blown
for ages and ages
the same wind
that blew across
a hollow reed
fifty-thousand
years ago
just as a man
was passing.

Marginalia

After transcribing scripture all day,
interrupted only by frequent prayer
or a Spartan meal, one would think
that those medieval monks would be anxious
to break out a little, to think outside the box,
or margins as the case may be. And they did.

After hours of drudgery copying Luke or Revelations,
after the day-in, day-out regimen of faith and devotion,
they strayed onto the edges of the parchment
and created something fanciful, a little *divertissement*
to amuse themselves—a snail with a cat's head,
an elephant imagined with a wolf's body,
a guy blowing a trumpet from his buttocks.

Then their pens would return to the realm
of rote and reason, as if nothing had ever happened,
as if imagination had never opened the borders,
but their smiles might last a little longer.

To a Famous Poet

You told us that you're terrible with names,
and if I or any of us met you
three months from now at an airport,
you might not remember us right away.
It's not memory loss, I'm sure,
just a constant parade of students
and admirers who spot you in a crowd—
frizzy mane, loose layers of skirts and scarves,
handcrafted jewelry, a smile that forgives
the absence of makeup,
the gentleness of years of Zen,
the Starbucks cup. You glide in and out
of busy lives like an earth-mother muse.
Some of us have been lucky enough
to work with you, absorb your wisdom,
have you sign our books, even receive
a hug goodbye, and we glow
with rubbed-off transcendence,
as you move off to another city
and another, meeting people who
pardon you for not remembering how
crossing your path has changed them.

Journal Evening (Loving Near June)

Let the summer simmer,
slice the melon and the lemon,
watch as he takes the steak
and grills it for the girls
and boys. Oh boy, don't waste sweat
on this afternoon—raft on one
lake or another, not hearing the hubbub.
Laze with zeal, find a breeze
and play on words, swordplay on paper.
Hang consonants, almost constant, on
wind chimes. Let no one chide your whims—
jumble letters, add and subtract.
We love solos—let loose vowels
in the air like fireflies. Life fries
us enough—let's relax, sell extra time,
emit happiness, eat, drink, trade ink,
write about summer, into the night thing
that brings mosquitoes, so some quit
to go inside, while we stand under stars,
sure strands of sky we understand.

Romantics

It's not some gilt-edged, bound-in-leather journal
in which I write with fancy flourishes,
my quill pen scratching odes to love eternal.

My Bic pen scrawls, its blue ink nourishes
lined paper bound by wire spiral spine,
torn cardboard covers held against their wishes

by duct tape, just to lend a silver shine.
What matters is what each of us discovers,
not whether your book's prettier than mine.

Let's read our work to our respective lovers
and see who swoons to each impassioned page,
and like the tiny hummingbird who hovers

around the nectar jar, their love will rage.
It's so much better than a living wage.

Interview with a Metaphor

Q: Why do you think you're so popular?
A: Because I am the sunflower to the honeybee.
I am the smell of rain that ends the drought.
I am the walk-off home run in the bottom of the ninth.

Q: Don't you think you sound a little full of yourself?
A: No, not at all.
When a writer's river of ink is flowing,
and he rides it in creativity's boat,
I am the sail turned into the wind of language.
It's just my job.

Q: But what do you say to those who believe
that metaphors are overused?
A: Can there be too many sunsets?
Did Mozart write too much music?
Can there be too much air to breathe?

Q: Can't a simile sometimes be just as effective?
A: The word "as" is the crutch of the weak-minded,
the badge of the bad aphorism,
the flag-bearer of weak analogies.

Q: Isn't that a bit harsh?
A: No, harsh is a pair of sandpaper briefs.

Q: Thank you for your time.
A: My pleasure. You are the call of curiosity
in the jungle of knowledge.

Archaics Roadshow

First of all, I'm amazed that this poem
was preserved so well for all these years
in your grandfather's attic.
Just look at the details in this piece:
Right here in the first stanza you have an "o'er,"
followed closely by a "twixt" and an "ere."

Then if you look carefully in the second stanza,
just below the "prithee," you'll see, very clearly,
a "betimes" and a "lackaday." I don't think
I've ever seen all three words in one stanza
in a poem of this vintage.

And finally, just as he finishes the last two lines,
the poet ends with a flourish: a "forsooth,"
a "wherefore" and a "twain."
What makes this such a valuable find
 is that the average poem of this era
may have had two or three archaic words—
this one has no less than nine.

The signature is authentic, and as I said,
it's in excellent condition. What's more,
the craftsmanship is remarkable—
they just don't make them like this anymore.
I think a poem like this could fetch
upward of ten thousand dollars.
Thank you for bringing it to us today.

Part II

Already Beginning to Heal

Mercurochrome Summer

The third time I skinned both my knees
the summer I was eight, my mother
just shook her head. "You'll have scabs
on top of your scabs," she sighed,
as she painted them both with Mercurochrome,
that vile, red liquid antiseptic that stung
worse than the scrapes themselves.
She eased my pain with a cherry Popsicle,
the sweet and cold in my mouth offsetting
the hot throbbing in my knees. Afterward,
I limped outside and showed Danny next door
my war-painted battle scars, then stuck out
my cherry-stained tongue, and told him
I drank some of the Mercurochrome.
"Yuck!" he cried.

It was a day full of red: Danny's big sister Julie
sashayed by to show off her new red sundress
and flip hairdo. I told her she looked like Sandra Dee,
but Danny said she smelled like onions. Later,
a fire engine screamed through the neighborhood
when Mr. Berry knocked over his barbecue grill
and set his lawn on fire. Fresh cut grass and charcoal
don't smell so good when they're put together.

I read in my science class that when the sun
goes down, the reds are the first colors to fade.
By dusk, my knees were no longer bright red,
and evening sounds took over for the colors—
the ice cream man on a late run, mosquitoes
teasing my ears, the Fisker brothers setting off
firecrackers in the woods, my parents watching
Jackie Gleason in the living room. I got ready for bed,

pulling my pajama pants over my tender knees,
which were already beginning to heal.

Shelter

It's to keep our family safe, my dad says.
I don't understand why we need another basement.
Mom buys 50 cans of vegetables, hoarding them for home.
Every day on TV they talk about the "Cold War,"
and it's not even wintertime. Dad shows me the new room.
There's just one door and no windows, and metal shelves
with cans of food, a transistor radio, blankets and flashlights.
There's powdered milk and bottled water too.
I guess that means the milkman won't leave bottles
on our porch if there's a war. Sometimes I dream about war,
sometimes I dream of Willie Mays. Dad says I worry too much
for a little child. Walking home from school, I watch the sky.
Sometimes I wish I was born in a UFO.

Aquaphobia

Perhaps it was the summer I was four—
a rogue wave swallowed me. One of my aunts
was there to pluck me out. "You'll live," she frowned.

Since then, big water's something I endure,
but never love. Can I swim? Not a chance,
nor do I sail—I'd rather stay aground.

Don't pity me my dry life—I'm content
away from lake and ocean, pond and sound.

But if there's some wet, desperate circumstance,
if some great flood falls from the firmament,
                              I'm drowned.

Hide and Seek

When she was a toddler,
she thought she could disappear,
so she just covered her eyes,
thinking if she couldn't see him
he couldn't see her.

Later, when she was three,
she always hid in the same spot,
and he would pretend to be stumped,
looking all around till he found her
in her favorite hiding place.

But soon she learned
to hide much better, to be stealthy,
always finding a different corner
in the bowels of the house,
especially when he came home drunk.

Science Fair Volcano

As a teacher, I've seen it many times—
the peaks of conical and homemade plaster
backed up by the obligatory signs.

It doesn't take a lot of skill to master
this impressive demonstration—inside
the peaks of conical and homemade plaster,

a vinegar-and-baking-soda bromide,
two strong conflicting forces that react—
an impressive demonstration inside

the gym. Fourth-grader Tyler did, in fact
create a project like this. Under pressure,
two strong conflicting forces did react,

exploding from his model house. He'd measure
all the damage done, but didn't keep a chart.
He made a science project under pressure

of a home about to blow itself apart.
The damage done, nobody kept a chart.
As a teacher, I've seen it many times,
backed up by the obligatory signs.

The Stars Obliterated

She looks up at the night sky, amazed
to see it so clearly. "In my city," she says,
"the sky is only gray—
all the city light washes out the stars."

She doesn't know the constellations,
so I point out Orion, sighting his belt,
the row of three bright stars, blue giants
from hundreds of light years away.

She doesn't know the mythology either,
so I describe his stature and heroism,
his hunting prowess, and how as Poseidon's son
he could walk on the ocean floor
with his head above the waves.

But he was a pig to women, I tell her.
He assaulted Merope after too much wine
and he pursued the Pleiades so relentlessly
that Zeus scooped them up for protection
and deposited them in the sky.

"That reminds me of something," she says,
but she will not share it,
and she is quiet for the rest of the night.

Things in Need of Love

after Sei Shōnagon

A broken wind chime. A robin with a broken wing.
A cluster of drooping tulips.
A stray dog who smells the air outside a steak house.
A family of eight in a one-bedroom apartment.

A man with an unwanted engagement ring.
A house with peeling paint. A city with a burning river.
A child sleeping under a Mylar blanket in a cage.
A man trying to sleep over a heating grate in the street,
his teeth still chattering.

A man who orders his seventh beer.
A man who has long ago forgotten why he is so angry now.
A woman in too much fear to leave her husband.
A veteran who wants to stop having nightmares.

An old woman who loses her way home.
A school whose children were murdered by guns.
A large country with a wedge driven into it.

Dewey-Eyed

A study cubby back behind the stacks
is where we first locked lips. The shelves between
the main desk and our tryst were filled, the racks
from Poetry to Fiction (811-813)

would camouflage shenanigans, while patrons turning pages
had no idea librarians could be their lusty selves,
bumping up against the books instead of earning wages,
pulling orders, organizing shelves.

And when we exited that private nook,
returning to the world of Mr. Dewey,
we might exchange a sideways smile or swap a furtive look,
but always being business-like, no sentimental hooey.

Then after work, like any learned lovers,
we'd read a book and get between the covers.

A Day in July

I won't apologize for the weather,
one of the hottest days of the summer.
I won't apologize for the venue either,
a little chapel on campus, not some
cavernous cathedral. I won't apologize
for our shoestring budget—the lack of a limo,
how we went to the reception in her dad's
old Pontiac, with her friend from next door
as chauffeur. I have no regrets for the music
I stayed up all night to tape, despite a lack
of tunes you could dance to. I'm not sorry
for the snafus—forgetting the marriage license,
her reciting my vows in her nervousness.
I won't even make excuses for the fact that
my fly was open through half of the reception.
All I know is the ends justify the means,
and looking back from a perspective
of forty-eight years, the day couldn't
have been more perfect.

Couch Nocturne

This spring day is drawing its curtain,
and a chilly breeze moves in to replace
the setting sun. Our dogwood is blooming
early this year, and the neighbor kids
are still playing street hockey.

You asked me half an hour ago
to take a walk with you, but now
you've nodded in front of *Dancing with the Stars,*
your head lolling to the left.
The sun has closed up shop, stars
are beginning to poke through the purple,
and you are snoring on the couch.
Another hard day. Maybe we are walking
through the neighborhood in your dreams,
talking about grandchildren, home renovations,
or how we need to get more exercise.

I don't have the heart to wake you.
We'll get another chance tomorrow.
But for now, they're doing the tango on TV,
and that couch looks so damned comfortable.

Trivia

Who was the first
How many
What is the word for
Who won
When did
Can you name the
Who is the only
In what year did
Where would you find
Which of these is
How many times
Where in the world did you
When did you think
What is the matter with
Why in God's name
What kind of question
How dare you
Do you expect me
Why should I
How am I supposed to
Who do you think you are?

Postcard to the Ex

There's a bear in the back yard
and piranhas in the kitchen sink.

The kids are dressing like clowns
and the bank took back the TV.

The car lost a wheel and a door.
Someone painted our windows black.

Your favorite chair caught fire,
and last night during the storm,

a huge tree limb crashed
through the bedroom ceiling

and onto your side of the bed.
Wish you were here.

Insidious

I am thinking of the tall trees,
and how beneath all the green distracting leaves
can lie rotted roots. I am thinking of the family
with eight kids, the ones always on TV,
and how indiscretions have finally bubbled up
all over the papers, jacking up their ratings.
I am thinking of my house, and how I don't know
if termites are turning the frame to sawdust.
I am thinking about the lion behind that boulder,
the drunk plowing through that red light,
the *e. coli* in that hamburger. I am thinking of
all the times I sat on the first-base line
and didn't get whacked in the forehead
by a line drive, and all the times I should have.
I am thinking about what's in the box.
I am thinking about what's under her dress.
I am thinking about riptides and covert operations,
insider trading and scratch-off lottery cards.
I am thinking about what I said to you last night,
and how like a cancer it was,
painless at first, but later destroying
all the good cells between us.

Public Apology

No one knows who paid for the message
that appeared in the deep blue air
over Brisbane that April day:

♡ U XX
I'm Sorry

The skywriter claims the customer was anonymous,
and for $4000 cash, he didn't press the issue.
Half an hour later, the characters were gone,
wisped away by the afternoon wind.
Who was that man, and what did he do
that would warrant a message more ephemeral
than roses, but indelible on the intended heart?

And how many lovers on the ground below,
trying to dig out from under a huge mistake,
took credit for that cloud-apology,
guaranteeing contentment in bedrooms
all over the city that night,
thanks to an act of contrition
written on the billboard of the sky?

What's Fixed

after Dorianne Laux

My car's transmission, its thin red serum
no longer seeping. Your pearl earring,

with a tiny drop of epoxy. My wrist, shattered
to an S-shaped monster of blood and bone,

bolted together to knit almost whole.
The garden hoe handle,

through the miracle of duct tape.
A friendship, torn apart by the lack

of a thank-you card, limping its way
back into the sun. A city, shaken down

and washed away by a vengeful earth,
re-collecting its pieces. And we,

under a reconciled moon, round again
if only for tonight, holding each other

together, our glue even stronger
than the thousand shards it mended.

The Agnostic's Sunday

Every weekend she flits about,
running late as usual, trying
to decide what dress to wear—
not that one with the itchy lace—
and wolfing down a quick breakfast,
usually a slice of raisin toast
with a spiral of cinnamon baked in.
She will quickly pin up her hair,
not worry about the chipped polish
on that one nail, kiss me goodbye,
and barrel out the door. I'll settle in
with my paper and orange juice, knowing
that she'll soon be in her pew,
summing up her life this week to God.
She will sing a few hymns, pray
to her favorite saints, go through
her mental list of loved ones
and say prayers for each of them,
and as if she thinks it would help,
save me for last.

PM

my
day unravels
like a sweater

until
your message
makes it better

you
send me
a virtual hug

it
sweeps despair
beneath my rug

while we're apart
emoji red heart

Part III

A Certain Age

The Man Peeling Sweet Potatoes
on Easter Morning

The man peeling sweet potatoes on Easter morning
looks frustrated, as though this is a task best passed
to others who really know what they are doing.
His wife is away on other errands and has deemed
him the stripper of skins, with nothing but a dull
vegetable peeler. Perhaps if he should microwave
them for five minutes, the dirt-brown husks
would pull away cleanly, even by tool-less hand.
The ends are hot and soft and peel more easily
but they burn his fingers, while the middle
is still too hard and resists a metal blade.
He is making a mess of this chore, and wonders
why his wife would entrust it to him, when he
could be watching baseball or writing poetry.
Perhaps today of all days he should have faith
that he will accomplish this goal of five pounds
of naked tubers, their bright orange souls
unprotected from the cruelties of the April air.
Sometimes it is easy to peel away defenses,
he thinks, and sometimes a toughness prevails.
Later, his wife will bake them in a casserole,
with cinnamon, brown sugar and marshmallow,
for a dinner that has taken three days to prepare,
and their aroma will rise from a hot square tomb
into the very reaches of Heaven.

Sette Pesci

My wife's side of the family celebrated
every Christmas Eve with a big spread
featuring seven fishes. No one knew
exactly what they represented, except
perhaps the Catholic concept of abstinence—
no meat on Fridays or holy days. No one
knew why seven either—maybe
for the seven sacraments,
the seven joys of Mary, or just
a lucky number.

They'd bring out the traditional Italian dishes—
baccalà, the salted cod we only pretended
to like, or *calamari, scungilli,* smelts.
Always there was shrimp cocktail,
usually crab legs, mussels marinara.
Sometimes there would be cheese pizza,
the fallback for seafood haters.

But as older folks passed on—those old enough
to be from Italy, or to know a relative who was—
we became more lax. Our kids grew up,
their likes and dislikes filtered into the buffet,
evolving into something else entirely—
the cod was the first to go. Truth be told,
nobody ever really liked those smelts either.
"And you know what *scungilli* really are, right?"
an uncle asked my kids. "Snails!"

So this Christmas Eve,
we've graced our groaning board
with unpeeled shrimp, crab cakes, tilapia,
little crackers that resemble goldfish,
tuna salad, sushi (in deference to my youngest,
the Japanophile), cheese pizza (half anchovies),
and out of respect for my second oldest,
who refuses to eat anything that swims,
a meatloaf shaped like a trout.

Rapids Again

By rights, we should be done with this.
We've already brought up three,
rode the whitewaters of their adolescence,
then walked them carefully through the door.
Now, when most of our peers are enjoying
grandparenthood, we are raising another,
rescued from the trap of a lesser life.
"He's blessed to have you," everyone tells us.
But at thirteen, he doesn't often feel that way.
Some days we feel too old to do this.
The rapids wait once again, rougher
than they ever seemed before.
But we're ready—our raft patched and inflated,
our life jackets strapped on tight,
our well-worn oars clutched in our hands.

Family Engagements

My wife's grandmother had one date
with her future husband, back when movies
were silent and a nickel. Its title is lost to the ages,
and they didn't even hold hands.
Her little brother and sister sat between them.
They were married over fifty years
and had four children.

One evening my wife's father came to visit
his friend, a fellow musician, and met his sister.
He wrote letters to her, and in one he said
that when he played his saxophone,
the music on his stand dissolved
and he would see her face.
They married six months before the war.

After a Christmas snowstorm, our son took his girlfriend
to see their favorite neighborhood lights display.
She turned around to brush some snow
off a lit plastic snowman, and when she turned back
he was on one knee.
He was married with his grandfather's wedding ring.

And I, the romantic poet,
proposed to my beloved, my wife of forty-eight years,
over the telephone.

Hoofing

Of the fifty-eight things I need to do before I die,
number six is to dance at your wedding.
Yes, me—the guy who once asked for the Virginia Reel
at my junior high dance, because I learned it in gym class
and it was the only dance I knew. I'll stumble and sway
with your mother and your bride through a slow dance,
but later I'll need at least three beers to lubricate
my creaky joints and my reserve, and a full dervish of guests
on the dance floor, a Brownian movement of bodies,
where I'll slip between Uncle Jack, who lumbers like
a grizzly bear, and Aunt Lois and her date, who have
inexplicably slid into a tango, while the flower girl
jumps randomly up and down, parachuting her petticoats.
I'll be a hoofer for you—
that is, I will dance like an animal without toes.
I won't do that damned Chicken Dance,
but I will bounce and celebrate to Kool and the Gang
or any of those obligatory songs, as this ecstatic mob
thrums along with abandon in a rented hall,
under a clear, rosy evening sky, where somewhere,
your grandmother does the tarantella.

Handyman

In this toddler's eyes, everything that comes apart
is broken, and she brings it to me—
"Fix it, Pop-Pop." It could be the torn page
from a picture book, or simply two building blocks
pulled apart. Once, a plastic Easter egg.

As far as she is concerned,
I am the world's greatest handyman.
Once on a walk, we saw a sidewalk slab
broken up and roped off for repair.
"Fix it, Pop-Pop," she said. I didn't have the heart
to tell her I don't do concrete work.

But I want to tell her this:
anything I can fix for you, I will.
If I could keep you from all the damages
of this world, I would.

How a Toddler Learns the Alphabet

A
book
carried around,
druidic runes on
each page,
fascinates her.
Grandpa reads, she
hears words.
In time,
just a little
knowledge
loosens the code:
mmm goes the M;
nothing is rounder than
O.
Picking them out,
quick study,
reading's not far away:
Snaky S goes *ssss*,
Tongue-staccato T.
Under the influence of
vocabulary,
wiser every day,
X marks the spot where a
young mind consumes with
zeal.

Easter Egg Hunt in a Church Graveyard

The irony of this is lost on three-
and four-year olds, who see this is a yard
with big stones in it. Basket-bearing, free,
they run for multicolored eggs. It's hard
for them, so parents help. Around the stones
they pluck their prizes, scampering above
the long departed, all the dust and bones
of those like Mary Wellington, beloved
wife, 1840-1892:
pneumonia, or some similar disease.
One wonders if she was a person who
had grandkids, and if so, she might be pleased
a little girl named Evie won the race
and found an egg above her resting place.

After Seeing *Star Wars*

after seeing *Star Wars* she says why is Dark Vader so bad and
I say you mean Darth Vader no she insists it's DARK Vader and
her young pink brain can be so set sometimes as she explains
he wears that black suit and he's so mean and he went to
the dark side so he's DARK Vader okay okay I concede you can
call him DARK Vader and anyway she says I just heard about
black holes and I'll bet Dark Vader lives in a black hole because
they say it's so black nothing can get out not even light but
I say if he went in he could never come out like a Roach Motel
what's a Roach Motel she asks never mind I say but maybe
she says he lives in a cave like Batman they call Batman the Dark
Knight so why can't there be a Dark Vader I can't dispute this
flawless five-year-old logic so I say you've got a point she
goes on I'll bet it's dark in the Batcave like a black hole except
Batman can come back out in his Batmobile why doesn't
Dark Vader have a Darkmobile let's go get ice cream I say

Senior Discount

Apparently, I've reached a certain age
where I'm forgiven at least ten percent.
I wonder how and when my youth was spent.

The movies, the museum, and the stage
all offer handsome discounts for this gent.
Apparently I've reached a certain age
where I'm forgiven at least ten percent.

Nobody checks ID, they simply gauge
me by my face and how my spine is bent.
Free coffee doesn't ease my discontent.

Apparently, I've reached a certain age
where I'm forgiven at least ten percent.
I wonder how and when my youth was spent.

Downsizing

Our green factories have closed for the season.
We've laid off all the chlorophyll,
let the carotene take over, putting in one last shift
as the days shorten and chill. Supple once,
our walls and stems crinkle at the edges,
turn crisp and brown. We hang on
till November winds strip us from security,
whip us through the frosty air. Unemployed,
we assemble on the ground, a crunchy crowd of castoffs
waiting for the inevitable, for the ones who will
sweep us up, herd us into piles to be bagged,
shredded, vacuumed, or God forbid, even burned.
But we are expendable, and the trees
are already rebuilding, waiting out the winter
for a new generation, a company of greenhorns,
young upstarts who will restart production
and cast their shadows against the necessary sun.

Papers on Top of More Papers

after "Black Stone Lying on a White Stone" by César Vallejo

I will die in a cubicle, on a sunny day,
a day as ordinary as any other, maybe in autumn.
I will die in a cubicle in the middle of a project
probably on a Tuesday, a day much like today.

It might be a Wednesday, come to think of it.
I will think it's writer's cramp, but it will spread
up my arm to my brain, the neurons exploding
like fireworks, my tongue lolling in my mouth.

Poor guy. Worked all his life. Maybe we shouldn't
have given him so much to do. Maybe we shouldn't
have used that cat-o'-nine-tails on him so much.

There are no witnesses, just the vacation posters
tacked to the inside walls of my space. And it's
a Tuesday or Wednesday, and it's just begun to cloud up.

Careful in the Fog

Our morning washed of details,
we move through a gray blanket—

our cars glide more quietly,
our morning washed of details.

Traffic lights come from nowhere.
Our cars glide more quietly.

Caution is our best defense:
traffic lights come from nowhere

at the last minute. We see
caution is our best defense

on this whitewashed workday.
At the last minute, we see

someone who wasn't careful
on this whitewashed workday.

Police strobe lights pierce the haze:
someone who wasn't careful.

Respectfully, we slow down;
police strobe lights pierce the haze.

We move through a gray blanket—
respectfully, we slow down.

Nail Pop

You little rebel,
poking your head above the floorboard,
who snagged my sock last week—
you're the cause of the hole in my sole.
Worse yet, you ripped the skin
on my wife's foot that same day.
I took a hammer and a nail-set punch
to you, banged you down subfloor
where you belong, only to find you
creeping aboveground again the next day.
I drove you down again, sealed you in
with a spot of glue, but you were made
of stronger stuff, and popped up
like a prairie dog two days later.
This morning, you bit my sock again,
the last straw. I grabbed a pair of pliers,
pulled you out like a bad tooth,
and plugged up your hole with wood filler.
Now no one knows you were ever there,
except now in your absence, the board,
a little looser, utters a ghostly squeak.

Deus ex Machina

I want the gods descending on a crane to bear me up
like in Greek tragedies, just when it seemed that all was lost
and certain death, or worse, dishonor, reared their ugly masks.

I want majestic eagles to swoop down and lift me up
securely in their talons, just like those in Middle Earth
who rescued Sam and Frodo from the red slopes of Mt. Doom.

I want a billionaire someday to knock upon my door
and say, "My friend, there's way too much for me to spend myself,
so take this cash to fix your roof and send your kids to school."

I want to hit the lottery, an unknown aunt to die
and leave me in her will. I want my dream job falling
in my lap, a fast machine to take me out of here

and land me in a tropic paradise, a margarita
in my hand. I want a happy ending to my story
no one would expect, that I didn't even have to earn.

Señor Morning

Age is a noisy leaf-blower at 7 a.m.
It's shiny red, gas-powered, and speaks in Russian.
When horizontal sun slices through my window
and coffee fumes climb the stairs,
I bury my face in a soft comforter
before I rise and plod to the bathroom.
Headache—I can hear the toothbrush and toothpaste
between my ears. My mouth is a car wreck of mint.
Like Hannibal in the Alps, my elephant-feet
clomp down the slope of the steps.
Really, I like the morning—it validates the fact
that I'm still alive. Who's making coffee, anyway?
I don't even like the stuff. Last night I dreamt that
everyone was saying "Twenty-three skidoo."
I think Roaring 20's slang gave me this headache.
Each day begins like a can of corn,
and I have to deal with the grumpy pit bull of aging.
Pop-Pop can break-dance and do the limbo.
Tomorrow he will free-climb El Capitan.
Is this possible? It won't matter someday soon,
when we will all clone ourselves at twenty-nine.
We will banish ugly beauty and progressive lenses.
Today, I wrestle with that monster *Weltschmerz*
while the mirror sticks out its tongue and razzes me.
But I'll get the last laugh when I blow away
like a leaf in the Russian wind.

Möbius Avenue

I step outside my house this evening, evaluating the stars and
my position. Off on another constitutional. It's always been exactly
one mile, but since they repaved the street, it's now twice as long.
It must be that strange pitch and roll, a half-twist about five blocks
down, that has changed things, left me strangely unsettled. My
perspective feels different, even though the stars, the trees and
houses look the same. The thing is, when I've gone two miles in a
straight line, I'm back at my own house. Another two miles, and it
happens again. And again. My street has become a tape loop,
a repeating echo, a real-life GIF. I am constantly leaving and
returning to my house at the same time. I feel a combination of
homesickness and wanderlust. Others I have encountered on my
street have the same puzzled expression that I must possess.
They don't know whether to be dismayed or reassured.

We're never too far from home, but we're never far enough.

Aprilcalypse, 2020

A light spring rain falls on Sunday morning
and the dandelions on my lawn.
I am here, not far from Independence Hall,
while democracy shakes like a leaf,
just as shaking hands is going out of style.
Squirrels dart across deserted streets
and tornados, my childhood nightmare,
rip through the South. This world can turn
on a dime, a dirty dime like the one I found
by the curb yesterday. From cornfields
to tenements, change is rattling the husks
and window panes. Some have spray painted
anarchy symbols and swastikas anonymously
in the alley by the trash cans; others boldly
brandish them on protest signs. My wife and I
watch the news looking for facts, while others
eat up Pizzagate and the Deep State,
jumping into a chasm of disinformation.
They fear Spanish and Chinese like I fear heights.
I grew up in a pink split-level, wear jeans
like Springsteen, build a playhouse for my grandkids
and read them *Goodnight Moon*. Now I have
a President who asks if we can inject disinfectant
to kill the virus in us, and I think of the film
Idiocracy. (Dear Mr. President, please sit down—
you're not helping. Very truly yours, a citizen.)
I wish I could just fly away from here, mount
a poetic Pegasus and lift us both into the clouds.
But solace will have to come from the real world,
like the empty boulevard lined with cherry trees
that bloom in the rain in my home town.

In the Bungalow of Colorful Aging

At first you feel as lost
as a marble after the game.

Your old bones rattle in their cage;
your feathers drop like November leaves.

But you refuse to dry up, to be a shell,
a metal casing with a hole inside.

Stretch yourself, be supple as rubber,
and stretch time too, a few more decades to rest

or be a kite, be a wolf in the snow.
Don't lose sight of your vision.

Forget the other world, where carrier pigeons
bring messages to nowhere,

and everyone you left behind
hitchhikes to the outskirts of regret.

Packing Old Records

The house has reached its saturation point,
so I pack old possessions for Goodwill,
my insignificant gesture of largess,
giving things I don't want to people I don't know.
I start to fill a box with old LPs.
My turntable has been disconnected for years,
and some of these I've already replaced
with their shiny, efficient descendants.

One album halts my progress—a band I haven't
thought about in years, one that the world has
passed by, a hippie folk band that had the temerity
to call themselves "Incredible," one we used to love.
We saw them at the Fillmore East in New York
when we were young and idealistic,
and we shared those liberated days and nights
as the turntable spun and the needle scratched out
songs with sitars and mandolins, about paint boxes
and caterpillars, inner light and the "first girl I loved."

The world's a darker place now, perhaps,
and our trajectories have split off, light years apart,
arcing into the lives and loves of others.
For another moment my hand hesitates,
then with a faint smile, I slide the record into the box,
wedging it into an array of well-worn cardboard spines.
It will probably become forgotten again,
but maybe it will become someone else's music.

Part IV

Look Out, Look Out, Look Out

When the Ghosts Came

When the ghosts came, we left them oatmeal on the kitchen table.
When the ghosts came, we left them three pairs of galoshes
    on the stairs.
When the ghosts came, we hung empty picture frames
    over the mantle,
cleaned our golf clubs,
and left out baseball cards for them to trade.

When the ghosts came, we made tents out of our bed sheets.
When the ghosts came, we left mousetraps in the cupboard.
When the ghosts came, we left the front porch light on,
 painted our windows blue,
and covered the mirrors with old horror movie posters.

When the ghosts came, we turned up the radio all the way.
When the ghosts came, we let the cat out and the dog in.
When the ghosts came, we read tarot cards,
got out the Ouija board,
and threw salt over our shoulders.

When the ghosts came, we banged on copper pots.
When the ghosts came, we hung papier maché owls
    from the chandelier.
When the ghosts came, we spread jam on the floor,
locked up the birdcages,
and put another log on the fire.

When the ghosts came, we painted our faces like tigers.
When the ghosts came, we sent red balloons
    out the nursery window.
When the ghosts came, we rolled up all the rugs,
waxed all our glass doorknobs,
and lit every candle in the house.

When the ghosts came, we were ready.
When the ghosts came, we were not ready.

Cedar

we inherited the house,
so we don't know the history of the tree
planted in a row with its brothers—

a windbreak, I think they call it—
a natural fence along our back property line
that has grown stories high over decades

but this one looks different—
the branches are dying, and little twigs
rain on the lawn after each storm

the trunk bows out from the ground
curving straighter as it reaches up
yet still looking precarious

the feathery leaves are sparser this year
than last, and if this giant decided to fall
it would slam right through our kitchen

when my wife was a child
one took out her swing set
moments after she left the seat

we talk about getting an arborist
sending little men to shimmy up the trunk
and trim it with knives and saws

perhaps right down to the stump
but meanwhile it looms over the yard
whispering:

I move slower than an hour hand
slower than moss
but faster than procrastination

look out, look out, look out

Randy Johnson Kills a Bird

March 24, 2001

Pity the unlucky dove that decided
to swoop down between home plate
and the mound, just as Johnson released
a ninety-mile-an-hour fastball.
Halfway between origin and destination
for both bird and ball, one could plot
the intersection of two curves,
one graceful and inverted,
one flattened out by sheer speed,
and at that intersection,
an explosion of feathers.

People laugh at the video today
but I'm sure Johnson was shaken up
when the bewildered ump called "No pitch!"
What else was there to do but clean up
the mess and continue the game?
The odds against such a meeting
were astronomical, but the universe
is a cruel and funny thing.
We plot our own parabolas every day
not really knowing what will intersect them -
drunk driver, aneurysm, asteroid.
All we can do is move along
and avoid fastballs when we can,
as we try to complete the arc.

Burying the Gerbil

First take a shoebox—children's size will do,
and gently place your fragile furry friend
inside, then pack with shavings and a few
small bits of kibble for his crypt. Pretend
you are a preacher—say a few kind words,
how he scurried on his wheel and seemed to smile
for lettuce, stuffed his cheeks and looked absurd,
the way he skittered on the kitchen tile
when he got out. Now find a proper place—
the rhododendron seems a pretty spot—
then say a creature's prayer and dig a space
just deep enough. Throw dirt into the plot,
then take the spade and hand it to your kid.
The gravel rattles on the cardboard lid.

Purple Heart

I gave away your clothes last week.
A truck rolled up and took six bags
to some forsaken warehouse where
they'd be passed on to people who

cannot afford to buy them new.
I gave away your clothes. Last week
I couldn't stand the closet full
of coats and dresses, hung like ghosts

and so I yanked them off their racks,
stuffed plastic bags with memories
I gave away. Your clothes, last week,
went to a world that never knew

how fine you were, how beautiful
in that red dress, that silken blouse
some stranger walks the street in now.
I gave away your clothes last week.

Last Spring

We looked out, Bill and I, from our balcony
on Tampa Bay. Below us, a Tiki bar clattered
with spring-breakers. Jet skis growled
and drew arcs in the bright water that reached
from our room to the ball park in Clearwater,
which hugged the horizon. We drove
the long causeway, mere feet above the bay;
had breakfast at Lenny's, teeming with Phillies fans;
then watched the game unfold with the afternoon—
blankets on the lawn beyond the right field fence,
where Florida sun baked us in mid-March,
and once, a home run ball dropped in to our left.
Later, we drove to the beach.
"One more thing off my bucket list," said Bill,
who hadn't told me he was feeling ill again,
as we walked the gentle surf of the Gulf
that seemed to stretch into forever.

Tribute to Flight 370

A prayer to the takeoff and landing of everything...
—Guy Garvey/Elbow

Here's to the beat of oscillating wings,
feathers turned into the wind,
the downward flap, the thrust and soar.

Here's to our weightlessness
as wheels lift off the tarmac, and engines
push into a corridor of sky.

Here's to updrafts and tailwinds,
gliding over canyons and lakes
above the sharp-beaked predator's eye.

Here's to Neil Armstrong and Superman,
and here's to the traffic helicopter,
the hummingbird's blur at the nectar jar.

Here's to coming down again,
tires chirping, talons clutching,
welcome rest, firm feel of home.

And here's to those who fell in the sea—
let's hope their souls have gone where
everyone lands where they want to be.

The Back Door

Heaven is a place where nothing ever happens...
　　　　　　　　　—Talking Heads

There are chaise lounges lined up to infinity
on a cloud like a cruise ship deck.
Some people are playing shuffleboard,
or ping-pong or mahjongg. Some people
are reading all the favorite books
they didn't have time for on Earth;
some are binge-watching old TV series.
There's a 24-hour buffet, and no one
ever worries about gaining weight.
There's a party in the community room,
and there's music playing but everyone hears
their own favorite music. I hear the Beatles.
People still make small talk, so no one knows
how they really feel, and everyone leaves
at eleven o'clock. There's a couple kissing
in the corner; they've been doing it all evening,
the same kiss over and over again.
A pretty woman who may have been a model
walks up to me and whispers,
"I've heard that Hell is more interesting."
So we slip out the back door to find out.

The Photo from M87

for Dr. Katie Bouman

When everything lined up—
your algorithm, the telescope signals—

when you displayed your array of hard drives,
dozens of them, all housing the bits and bytes
and years needed to accomplish this historic task—

when the photo went viral, a fiery iris
around an utterly black pupil, and people
called it many things, like "The Eye of Sauron"—

when we all realized we were staring at
a black hole, 55 million light-years away,
that we were looking into the darkest, densest
power of the universe, where everything
may go in the end, and we realized that you,
a woman not quite thirty (young enough
to be my daughter), were able to bring it to us
from those mind-blowing reaches of space,
and the camera caught you watching a monitor
as the image finally assembled,
and you held your hands to your mouth,
trying in vain to contain your unbridled joy—

that's the kind of joy I want.

About the Author

Bruce W. Niedt is a retired "beneficent bureaucrat" who began writing poetry again in 1999 after a long hiatus. Since then he has had over two hundred poems published in dozens of online and print journals, including *Rattle, Writer's Digest, Mason Street Review, Boston Literary Magazine, Tiferet, Spitball, Chantarelle's Notebook, US 1 Worksheets, The Lyric, Edison Literary Review, Star*Line,* and *Your Daily Poem.* His work has also appeared in the anthologies *Best of the Barefoot Muse, Poem Your Heart Out,* and *Ice Cream Poems.* He has won poetry awards from *ByLine Magazine, Writer's Digest,* and the Philadelphia Writers Conference, as well as three Pushcart Prize nominations and two Best of the Net nominations. He has had the good fortune to participate in poetry workshops led by Billy Collins, Jane Hirshfield, Marge Piercy, Molly Peacock, and a host of others. He has published seven poetry chapbooks, most recently *Hits and Sacrifices* (Finishing Line Press, 2016) and *Aprilcalypse* (Four Feathers Press, 2020). This is his first full-length poetry collection.

A graduate of Rutgers University, he is a proud father of four and grandfather of three, and lives with his loving and incredibly patient wife in Cherry Hill, NJ. An avid game show and trivia aficionado, he has appeared twice as a contestant on *Who Wants to Be a Millionaire?,* but *Jeopardy!* is still on his bucket list.

www.ingramcontent.com/pod-product-compliance
Lightning Source LLC
Chambersburg PA
CBHW031149090426
42738CB00008B/1270